SPANISH FOOD PHRASE BOOK & DICTIONARY

By: Mike Sealey

Copyright 2015

This phrase book and dictionary is compiled with the assistance of the Spanish MERCADONA supermarket chain.

Important Note: The content of this book is based on Castilian Spanish (*castellano*), the official Spanish language. A minority of Spain may use regional dialects/languages in some areas of the provinces of Catalonia, Valencia, Galicia and the Basque Country, which do not correspond to the following Castilian vocabulary.

Handy phrases in the restaurant refers to items in common use. The phrases and words therein do not attempt to translate the dishes which are uniquely inventions of the restaurant.

SECTION 1: Spanish - English

Table of Contents

Pronounciation guide…………………………..7

Poultry………………………………………………….9

Beef……………………………………………………..11

Pork…………………………………………………...13

Ham…………………………………………………….15

Lamb…………………………………………………..16

Prepared Meat Products……………………17

Fish…………………………………………………….19

Seafood……………………………………………...22

Vegetables………………………………………....25

Fruit……………………………………………………29

Rice &

Pulses………………………………..**31**

Bakery Products…………………………….**33**

Dairy Products……………………………….**36**

Spices……………………………………..**39**

Nuts…………………………………………..**42**

Drinks & Refreshments……………………….**44**

An Alcoholic Special………………………..**49**

Useful Words & Phrases at the shops…..**53**

Handy phrases in the restaurant…………..**57**

Cooking or Preparation Instructions…….**66**

SECTION 2: English - Spanish

Fish - *Pescado*…………………………………….73

Seafood and Shellfish - *Mariscos*…………..75

Poultry - *Aves, pollería*………………………..77

Beef - *Ternera*…………………………………..79

Pork and Ham - *Cerdo y Jamón*……………81

Lamb - *Cordero*…………………………………..84

Prepared Meats - *Carnes Preparadas*……..85

Vegetables - *Verduras*………………………..86

Fruit - *Frutas*……………………………………89

Rice and Beans - *Arrozes y Alubias*……….92

Bakery - *Panadería*……………………………..93

Dairy Foods -………………………………………..96

Spices - *Especias*…………………………..….99

Nuts - *Nueces*………………………………..…102

Drinks and refreshments - *Bebidas y Refreshments*…………………………….….103

Supermarket - *Supermercado*………………107

Restaurant - *Restaurante*………………....112

Spanish Pronunciation Guide

a - as in c**a**r, *b* - as in **b**erry, *c* - as in **th**ing (when before the letters 'i' and 'e'), *ch* - as in **ch**urch, *d* - as in **d**ate, *e* - as in h**ay**, *f* - as in **f**ruit, *g* - as in **g**reat (before all letters except 'e' and 'i' when it sounds like a throaty 'h'), *h* is silent, *i* as in t**ea**, *j* like a throaty '**h**', *k* as in tra**ck**, *l* as in **l**ip, *ll* double l sounds a bit like **li**ason, *m* sounds like **m**um, *n* sounds like **n**ut, *ñ* sounds like **ny** (e´g. Pe**ñ**on is pronounced Pe**ny**on), *o* as in p**o**nd, *p* as in **p**en, *q* as in **k**ite, *r* is rolled on the tongue, *rr* is a long roll on the tongue, *s* as in **s**uit, *t* as in **t**able, *u* as in fl**u**te,

v as in **v**ery, *w* is not in the Spanish alphabet but is occasionally used as in borrowed English. e.g. Windows (Microsoft), *x* as in e**x**act, *y* as in **y**es, *z* as in **th**ong.

<u>**Notes**</u>: the letter '*v*' may often be pronounced like a 'b' so that the town of **V**alencia is often spoken like **B**alencia.One of the most useful words in the Spanish language when asking for something is *hay,* pronounced like the British words **eye** or **aye**. It is useful because it can mean, **Is there any?** or **Are there any?** when used with an interrogative intonation. E.g. *Hay leche?* **Is there any milk?** *Hay uvas?* **Are there any grapes?**

The answer in the affirmative is simply, *Si, hay* meaning

yes, there is or **yes, there are.**

The answer in negative is simply, ***No hay*** meaning **No there isn't** or **No there aren't.**

Hay, a word that is easy to use and saves a lot of grammar study.

Poultry

Chicken, *pollo*. Duck, *pato*. Turkey, *pavo*.

Simply substitute *pato* or *pavo* for *pollo* where applicable in the phrases below according to the meat you require.

Alas de pollo, chicken wings

Ave, general term for poultry or bird

Entremusculos de pollo, chicken thighs

Gallina, hen

Pollo entero, whole chicken

Pollo entero limpio, whole oven ready chichen without innards, head or feet.

Pechuga de pollo, chicken breast

Pechuga de pollo, filetada, sliced chicken breast

Pechuga de pollo entera, whole chicken breast

Pollo troceado (or *trocitos de pollo*), chopped chicken, prepared for cooking *Paella*

Hígado de pollo, chicken livers

Traseros de pollo, leg quarters,

Jamoncitos de pollo, chicken legs

Solomillo strips of tender chicken (ideal for chopping up into small bits to make a stir fry or cooked as they are with a tasty mushroom sauce).

Pollo asado, roast chicken

Codornices, those little chickens are quails.

Oca, goose

Faisán, pheasant

Perdiz, partridge

Beef - *Ternera*

Albondigas de ternera, beef meatballs

Bistec, beef steak

Bovino, general term for cattle meat

Callos, tripe

Costillas de ternera, beef ribs

Entrañas is meat from the region of the diaphram. A very yummy cut of meat but can also be translated as 'entrails' which is a bit of a turn-off

Entrecote, Hmmm! I think we all know this one

Entrecote de lomo, topside steak from the back

Filetes de ternera, fillet steak

Hamburguesas de ternera, beefburgers

Morcillo, shank of beef

Ossobucco, meaty leg bone slice

Rabo(de buey), oxtail

Rabo(de buey), oxtail

Rosbif, roast beef (sometimes found prepared in slices at the cold counter); the cut used for a traditional English roast is not typical of Spanish cooking. So, if you are self-catering and missing a spot of ye olde home cooking on a Sunday, this is the phrase you need to ask the butcher: ***Un trozo de ternera para asar, estilo Inglés***.

Solomillo, sirloin steak

Salchichas de ternera, beef sausage

Ternera picada, minced beef***Ternera para guisar***, stewing steak

Ternera para freir, beef for frying

Vaca, cow

Vacuno, another term often used for beef; most often with minced meat or hamburgers

Vacuno/cerdo, is used on labelling to denote minced

meat which is a mix of beef and pork

Pork

Albondigas de cerdo, pork meatballs

Bacón, bacon (that's an easy one). Sometmes spelled *beicón*

Bacón ahumado, smoked bacon

Cerdo, pig, pork

Chuletas de cerdo, pork chops

Chuletas de aguja, Succulent shoulder cut pork chops and less expensive

Costillas de cerdo, pork ribs

Cerdo picada, pork mince

Cinta de lomo,

Higado de cerdo, pig's liver

Lomo de cerdo cut of pork loin

Magro, loin cuts or can   simply mean 'lean

Panceta de cerdo, belly pork

Panceta de cerdo, belly pork

Pincho moruno, skewered pieces of marinaded pork. Sometimes called **pinchito**

Porcino, Porcine, a general term for porky products sometimes used on labelling

Riñones de cerdo, pig's kidneys

Secreto de cerdo, literally 'pigs secret'. A prize cut of belly pork close to the shoulder.

Salchichas de cerdo, pork sausages

Torreznos, pork crackling

Ham

Jamón, ham. (*Jamón York*, York ham)

Jamón Serrano, the most famous of all Spanish legs of ham

Jamón Serrano hembra, Same as previous but from a female pig

Jamón Iberico, Similar to Serrano but from black pig and is more expensive.

Jamón Iberico de bellota, from black pig fed on its favourite food, acorns. Very expensive. Look for the word *bellota-* acorn

Jamón de cebo, fed on fodder

Jamón de la pata, ham off the bone

Jamón al horno, another term often used for ham off the bone

Lacón, another term for shoulder pork off the bone

Paleta ibérica, shoulder pork Iberian style

Lamb

Cordero, lamb

Chuletas de cordero, lamb chops

Cuello de cordero, neck of lamb

Pierna de cordero, leg of lamb

Other meat products

Cabrito, kid goat

Cabra, that tough old lamb is a goat

Conejo, rabbit

Prepared Meat Products

Butifarra, a kind of sausage

Chorizo, semi-hard seasoned pork sausage

Embutidos, general term for sausage-like products in a sausage-like skin

The Spanish are big on sausages with many regional variations; and they're a lot tastier than skinfuls of water with breadcrumbs

Embuchado, dry cured pork stuffed in a tripe skin

Fuet, spìcy sausage

Longaniza, pork sausage made with spices

Morcilla, similar to black pudding

Mortadela, pork meat compressed into a roll

Pelota, A large oval (pork) meatball made with garlic and parsley; often served in a lettuce or cabbage leaf wrap

Pinchos morunos, pieces of meat on a skewer

Preparados barbacoa, ready to cook on the barbeque

Salchichón, spicy sausage similar to salami

N.B. Lots of alergic people steer well clear of prepared sausage meats because they may well contain sulphides, gluten, soya, lactose, or its derivatives. If you enjoy the taste of prepared sausage meats there is a producer that claims to make such products free of allergens; look for the name of Casa Duran on the labelling.

Fish

Pescado, fish that's been fished but it's a *Pez* if it is still swimming about in the water

Anguila, eel

Angulas, tiny eels (see also *gula*)

Anchoa, anchovy (see also *bcquerones*)

Atún, tuna

Atún en aceite girasol, tuna in sunflower oil (tinned tuna)

Atún en aceite vegetal, tuna in vegetable oil

Boquerones, anchovies (see also *anchoa*)

Bonito, another word for tuna

Bacalao, cod

Chanquetes, whitebait

Camerones, shrimps

Dorada, a type of bream

Emperador, swordfish

Gula, a dish of tiny eels

Lenguado, sole

Lubina, sea bass

Melva, a species of tuna

Merluza, hake

Mero, grouper

Mojarra, a kind of sea bream

Panga, a cheap fish often served for school lunches

Pescadilla, whiting or young hake

Pez espada, swordfish

Rodaballo, turbot

Rodaja de salmón, salmon sliced into thick roundels

Rape, (pronounced **'Ra-pay'**) monkfish

Salmón, salmon (and no prizes for guessing this one either)

Sardina, if you guessed 'sardine', you were right.

Sardinillas, little sardines

Tollo (sometimes called *toya),* a species of shark

Trucha, trout

Seafood

Almeja, clam

Berberechos, cockles

Bogavante, lobster

Buey del mar, a big edible crab

Calamar, squid

Chiperones, baby cuttlefish

Chopitos, baby squids

Calamar a la romana, squid fried in batter

Carabineros, large red prawns

Cangrejo, crab

Cigalas, crayfish (see also *Langostino de rio*)

Erizo, sea urchin

Gambas, prawns or shrimps

Gambón grande, big prawns

Gambón gigante, even bigger prawns

Gambas peladas, peeled praw

Gambas crudas, uncooked prawns

Gambas cocidas, cooked prawns

Huevas, fish spawn but in Latin America the word often means testicles.

Langostino, big daddy king prawns

Langostino de rio, crayfish

Langosta, another word for lobster (see also *Bogavante*)

Marinero/a, a collective word for a seafood preparation

Mariscos, seafood in general. Very popular in Spain for a traditional Christmas family dinner

Mejillones, mussels

Mejillones en escobeche, pickled mussels

Mejillones, mussels

Mejillones en escobeche, pickled mussels

Muslitos de cangrejo, crab claws

Navajas, razor shellfish

Ostras, oysters.

Percebes, goose barnacles. A delicacy from the rocky northern coasts; difficult to collect and quite a risky business so they are expensive.

Pulpo, octopus

Sepia, cuttlefish

Vieira, scallop

Vegetables

Strictly speaking of course, the beans included here are known as pulses but lots of us think of them as vegetables

Alcachofa, artichoke

Apio, celery

Alubias, beans

Alubias rojas, kidney beans

Aceitunas, olives

Acelgas, Swiss chard

Aguacate, Avocado

Berenjena, aubergine

Boniato, sweet potato

Brecól, broccoli

Calabacín, courgette

Cebolla, onion

Cebolla tierna, spring onion

Col, cabbage

Coliflor, cauliflower

Champiñones, mushrooms

Espárragos, asparagus

Espinacas, spinach

Endiva, endive

Frijoles, dried beans

Garrofón, butter beans

Garbanzos, chick peas

Guisantes, peas

Habas, broad beans

Judias, green beans

Judias anchas, broad beans

Lechuga, lettuce

Judias anchas, broad beans

Lechuga, lettuce

Legumbres, vegetables (see also *verduras*)

Maiz dulce, sweet corn

Nabo, turnip

Nabo sueco, swede (literally means a Swedish turnip)

Puerro, leek

Patata, potato

Piñon, pine kernal

Pisto, similar to ratatouille (fried vegetables in a tomato sauce)

Pimiento rojo, red pepper

Pimiento verde, green   pepper

Remolacha, beetroot

Repollo, cabbage

Repollito de Bruselas, Brussel sprouts (a term more common in Latin America)

Seta, a variety of mushroom

Tomate, tomato. **Rama de tomatos** is tomatos sold on a twig.

Tomate triturado, tomato that has been pulped into little bits

Tomate frito, a cooked tomato sauce used for cooking

Verduras, the collective word for vegetables

Vegetal, used to describe cooking oil or food products derived from vegetables

Zanahoria, carrot

Fruit

Albericoque, apricot

Arándano, cranberry

Ciruela, plum

Cereza, cherry

Chirimoya, custard apple

Frambuesa, rasberry

Fresa, strawberry

Granada, pomegranate

Grosella, redcurrant

Grosella espinosa, gooseberry

Guayaba, guava

Kaki, caqui

Kiwi, kiw1

Lima, limei*Lima,* lime

Limón, lemon

Manzana, apple

Melocotón, peach

Melón, melon

Mora, blackberry

Naranja, orange

Nectarina, nectarine

Pera, pear

Piña, pineapple

Plátano, banana

Pomelo, grapefruit

Sandía, watermelon

Toronja, another word for grapefruit

Uva, grape

Rice and Pulses

Alubias, beans

Arroz, rice

Arroz integral, brown or wholemeal rice

Arroz de grano largo, long grain rice

Arroz redondo, round grain rice

Alubias blancas, butter beans

Frijol(es), haricot beans

Garbanzo, chickpea

Garrofón, white beans, butter beans

Habas, broad beans

Judias, green beans

Lentejas, lentils

NB. Although there are specific Spanish terms for kidney beans, butter

beans, etc. they may all be classed as *alubias* or *frijoles* or *alubias blancas(white beans)* so if you see them on a restaurant menu you might have to take pot luck with what comes out on your plate.

Bakery Products

Barra, a stick of bread similar to the French baguette

Barra integral, wholemeal baguette

Berlinas, doughnuts

Bollería, general term for pastries

Brioche, a cake confection. Literally means a 'brooch'.

Chapata, a type of bread roll

Con semillas, with seeds

Croisant, same as the French **croissant** as is used in English

Dulce, any pastry that is sweet tasting, i.e. cakes

Empanadilla, pasty

Empanadilla de tomate, tomato pasty

Empanadilla de atún, tuna pasty

Empanadilla de cebolla,   onion pasty

Empanadilla de espinacas, spinach pasty

Hojaldre, puff pastry

Mona, bun cake traditional at Easter

Pan, bread

Panadería, bakery

Pan integral, wholemeal bread

Pan cortado, cut or sliced bread

Pan sin corteza, bread without crusts

Pan de molde, a regular loaf of bread

Pan de leche, milk bread that's softer than the crunchy *barra*

Panecillo, bread rolls or buns

Pan sin corteza, bread without crusts

Pastel, any kind of cake confection (but can also be used for meat pies)

Roscón, a circular cake that is popular at festivals.

Tarta, tart or pie,

Tarta de manzana, apple tart

Tarta de carne, meat pie. Sometimes known as **pastel de carne**.

Trigo, wheat flour

Dairy Products

Huevos, eggs

Huevos camperos, free range eggs

Leche, milk

Leche entera, whole milk

Leche semi-desnatada, semi-skimmed milk

Leche desnatada, skimmed milk

Leche con calcio, calcium enriched milk

Leche condensada, condensed milk

Mantequilla, butter

Mantequilla sin sal, unsalted butter

Mantequilla con sal, salted butter

Nata, cream

Nata para montar, pouring cream for desserts *Nata para cocinar,* cooking   cream

Queso, cheese

Yogur, yoghurt

Queso, cheese

NB. Cheeses are usually recognized by their original names like Roquefort, Chedder etc. but the following are descriptive terms

Azul, blue

Curado, cured

Semi-curado, semi-cured

Cremoso, creamed

Con hierbas, with herbs

Con nueces, with nuts

De untar, for spreading

De cabra, from goat's milk

De oveja, made from sheep's milk

Duro, hard

Fresca/o, fresh (sometimes used for cheese similar to cottage cheese

Gratinado, grated as often used as a pasta topping

Lonchas, slices

Mezcla, mixed

Rallado, grated cheese

Sabor intenso, strong flavoured

Tierno can mean mild, young, fresh or tender in a cheesy kind of way

Spices

There are hundreds of varieties of spices and seasonings but these are the ones most likely to be used in Spanish cuisine

Albahaca, basil

Ajo, garlic (**diente de ajo** - garlic clove)

Ajo en polvo, powdered garlic

Ajonjoli, sesame

Azafrán, saffron (essential paella seasoning)

Cardamomo, cardamom

Canela, cinnamon

Canela en rama, cinnamon stick

Chili, chilli

Chili en polvo, chilli powder

Cilantro, coriander

Cominos, cumin seeds

Cominos, cumin seeds

Clavos, cloves

Cúrcuma, turmeric

Especias, spices

Enaldo, dill

Estragón, tarragon

Ginebre, ginger

Hierba buena, herbs with mint

Hierbas provenzales, a herb mixture of oregano, sage, rosemary, & thyme

Laurel, bay leaf

Menta, mint

Mostaza, mustard

Nuez moscada, nutmeg

Orégano, oregano

Perejil, parsley

Pimienta, pepper

Pimienta en grano, peppercorns

Pimienta negra, black pepper,

Pimentón dulce, sweet paprika

Pimentón picante, hot paprika

Romero, rosemary

Salvia, sage

Sal (de mesa) table salt (not strictly a spice but good to know if you avoid salt)

Tomillo, thyme

Nuts

Almendras, almonds

Anacardo, cashew

Avellana, hazelnut

Cacahuetes, peanuts

Cascara, shell. *Sin cascara*, without shell.

Coco, coconut

Coquito, brazil nut, or *nuez de Brasil*

Castañas, chestnuts

Macadamia, macadamia

Nogal, walnut

Pacana, pecan

Pistacho, pistachio

NB. Words applicable to nut preparations:

Con miel, honey coated

Con sal, salted

Tostado, toasted

Drinks and refreshments

Agua, water

Agua con gas, fizzy water

Agua sin gas, still water in the non-fizzy sense of the word

Batido, milkshake (see fruits for varieties)

Bebida, drink in general (or drunk if you're female and had too much; ***bebido*** if you're a male). Another less polite word for 'drunk' is ***borracho***

Botellín, a small bottle (usually 1/5th litre)

Café Americano, regular black coffee

Café BonBon, a small dark coffee made with condensed milk

Café, coffee

Café con leche, coffee with milk

Café descafeinado, decaffinated coffee

Café espresso, small strong shot of coffee

Café irlandesa, Irish coffee

Café con gotas, Lit. coffee with drops (i.e. coffee with a few drops of licquor of choice)

Café solo, small strong coffee

Carajillo, another word for coffee with a splash of brandy or other licquor

Casera, a carbonated drink similar to lemonade

Cortado, a smaller, stronger version of **café con leche**

Caña, beer out of the barrel

Cerveza, beer

Cerveza sin (alcohol), non-alcoholic beer

Copa (una copa de), a glass of (used for alchohol)

Cubatas, rum & coke (**Cuba libre**)

Granizado, a summer drink made with fruit syrup in a base of crushed ice

Horchata, a healthy drink made from tigernut milk and served ice cold

Infusión, tea (usually a variety of different teas on offer)

Infusión de manzanilla, chamomile tea

Ifusion de tila, lime blossom tea

Leche, milk (see dairy products for varieties)

Leche de soja, soya milk

Refresco, general term for refreshment

Taza, cup

Té. Tea

Té verde, green tea

Tercio de cerveza, 33ml bottle of beer (lit. a third of beer)

Vino, wine

Vino blanco, white wine,

Vino rosado, rosé

Vino tinto, red wine

Vino de la casa, house wine

Vino seco, dry wine

Vino dulce, sweet wine

Vinagre, vinegar; not a drink but could be used to describe some house wines

Zumo, juice (see fruit & veg. for varieties)

Zumo de naranja exprimido, freshly squeezed orange juice

Useful phrases when ordering drinks:

Frío, cold

Sin hiélo, without ice

Con hiélo, with ice

Caliente, hot

Largo de café, when you want a strong white coffee. You could also say **café fuerte**

Largo de leche, when you want a milky white coffee

Jarra, carafe or jug

Templado, warm or in the case of wine - room temperature (in the summer many Spanish bars serve red wine from the fridge).

De tiempo is also commonly used when referring to wine.

An Alcoholic Special

Queimada Gallega. This is a potent, fiery concoction with origins cloaked in the rural mystery of the northern province of Galicia. It is made in a large earthenware pot like a mini-cauldron and best drunk in small quantities (no pint glasses then) at the stroke of midnight on special nights such as Halloween or New Years Eve. If you're at a party it's handy to have a white witch among the guests because there's a mystical incantation, translated below from the original Galician dialect, which should be recited over the brew. ***Agua Ardiente*** (Firewater) as it is called is the main ingredient of the concoction and it is usually available under the name of ***Oruja.*** The elements of Earth and Water are represented by the Pot and the Agua Ardiente; the Fire is for purification and the Air is where the flames dance. In the context below, 'Holy Company' refers to the 'Parade of the Dead'.

Owls, night birds, toads and witches

Demons, goblins and devils.

Spirits from the misty vales;

Crows, salamanders and midges

The magic hex of sorcerers.

The putrid hollows of dead trees;

Home to worms and bloodsuckers.

Wisps of the Holy Company.

The evil eye and black magic spells,

The stink of the dead, thunder and lightning.

The howl of dogs that heralds death.

Satyr's snout and cloven hoof;

Sinful tongue of an evil crone

Betrothed to an ancient man.Satan's hell and Beelzebub,

Flames of burning corpses.

The mutilated forms of shameless wretches

And the pungent fumes from hellish sphincters.

The roar of a raging sea,

The barren wombs of spinsters;

The howl of cats on heat and

The stinking hair of a stillborn goat.

May these bellows fan life to

The flames of this fiery brew to

Simulate those of Hell

And that witches, straddling

Their broomstick steeds, flee

To cleanse their souls in theQuagmire sands of some

foresaken beach.

Oh hark the screams of   *pain*

Of those who burn in the fiery water

As they become purified.

And when this brew courses down our throats

We ourselves shall be cleansed of evil

And be free of sorcery and withcraft.

May the forces of fire, earth and water

Heed our cries for verily their powers

Are greater than those of man.

Here, now, and together,

Let the spirits of our absent friends

Join with us in this ritual burning.

Useful words and phrases at the shops

A typical exhange at the butchers counter might be, for example:

Butcher, *'Que le pongo?'* (He or she is asking what you would like. Lit. What shall I put you.)

Customer. *Pon me un pollo entero limpio por favor. (*A whole oven ready chicken, please.)

Butcher. *'Algo más?'* (Anything else?)

Customer. *'Sí, una pechuga de pavo'* (Yes, a turkey breast or substitute *pavo* for whatever you may need) or **'*No, gracias'*** (No, thank you)

Or, simply say *Todo* which would mean 'That's all'

If you look for something you cannot find in a supermarket, a useful phrase is '***Donde está...........?'***, Where is.......?

Abre facíl, easy to open.*Aceite de girasol*, sunflower oil

Aceite de oliva, olive oil

Ahumado/a, smoked

Brochetas, food skewered on a stick

Caldo, soup or broth

Caldo de carne, beef stock

Caldo de verduras, vegetable stock

Caldo de pollo, chicken stock

Caldito, stock or soup dehydrated

Cocido/a, cooked

Consumir preferentemente antes del……. eat preferably before…….. (date as shown)

Conservar en lugar fresco y seco, store in a cool, dry place

Contiene nuezes, contains nuts

Gluten, contains gluten or   **contiene gluten**

Sin gluten, gluten free (without gluten)

Curado/a, cured

Envasado al vacio, vacuum packed

Fecha de caducidad, sell by date

Granel, fruit or vegetables etc. sold loose as opposed to pre-packaged

Horno, oven (*Al horno* - oven cooked)

Laminado, sliced products (tinned mushrooms for example)

Lavado, washed (potato for example)

Levadura, baking powder

Lonchas, slices

Lonchas finas, thin slices

Lonchas gordas, thick slices

Microonda, microwave

57

Migas, small pieces, shreds

Panecillos, bread rolls or buns

Pelado, peeled (as often seen on tins)

Ración, ration or helping

Rellena/o, stuffed, e.g. **aceitunas rellenas de atún,** olives stuffed with tuna

Relleno, stuffing (English style chicken is sold in some supermarkets)

Sin colorantes artificiales, without artificial colourings

Sin conservantes artificiales, without artificial preservatives

Soja, soya

Trozo, trozito, slice as in a slice of cake or similar

Vinagre, vinegar

Una vez abierto conservar enelfrigorifico,once opened store in refrigerator

Handy words and phrases in the restaurant

La carta, the menu. (**N.B**. The Spanish word *menú* refers to 'dish of the day' in some restaurants)

Platero, a dish of food prepared and chosen by the house.

Plato del Día, dish of the day

Todos los platos llevan incluido....., all of the dishes include...(fries, salad or etc.)

Una mesa para 2 (3, 4 etc.), a table for 2 (3, 4 etc.)

(Uno, one, *dos*, two, *tres*, three, *cuatro*, four, *cinco*, five, *seis*, six, *siete*, seven, *ocho*, eight, *nueve*, nine, *diez*, ten)

Quiero reservar una mesa, I want to reserve a table, eg.*A las ocho, (a las nueve, etc),* at eight o'clock, (at nine o'clock etc.)

Buen proveche, bon apetit, enjoy your meal

La cuenta por favor, the bill please

IVA incluido, Value Added Tax (VAT) included

Pago con tarjeta, I'll pay with a credit card

Una cubierta por favor, a knife and fork please.
Cubierta is the collective word for the usual eating utensils. The individual words are: *cuchillo*, knife, *tenedor*, fork, *cuchara*, spoon.

No gracias, he comido sufficiente, No thank you, I've eaten enough

Camarero/a, waiter/waitress

Useful vocabulary commonly found on menus. This is not a comprehensive list because the inventiveness of restaurants throughout the world produces dishes with house names that will not be found in any dictionary. Some of vocabulary below may prove useful at the dinner table. Basic ingredients of meals may be found under the foregoing food sections

Acompañadas de, accompanied with

Arroz negro, black rice cooked in the ink of a squid or cuttlefish

Asado, roasted

Al ajillo, with garlicky sauce

A la brasa, chargrilled

A la parilla, grilled on a grid

A la plancha, grilled (usually on a hot plate)

A la barbacoa, barbecued

A la sidra, cooked with cider

Alitas de pollo, chicken wings

Bien hecho, or *bien cocido,* well cooked (*Crudo,* underdone)

Bife, steak cooked on a hot plate. Sometimes means minute steak

Bolsito/a de, a parcel of (e.g. a food item wrapped in a pastry casing)

Café irlandese, Irish coffee

Casero/a, home made

Cazuela, casserole

Cebollino, shallot (a word sometimes used for small onion or spring onion)

Chistorra, fish basket

Codillo de cerdo, pigs trotters

Cogollos, the tender inside parts of vegetables

Comida típica, typical regional dish

Crema de queso, cream

Gratinado, au gratin

Crudo, raw

Crujiente, crunchy or crispy

Desayuno, breakfast

Ensaladilla, salad

Ensaladilla Rusa, Russian   salad

Entremeses, appetizers, hors douvres

Entrantes, starters

Estofado, stew

Fideos, a dish made with fine pasta noodles (sometimes called *fidua*)

Flautas, food wrapped in tacos or a pastry casing

Guarnación, garnishing

Hojaldre, puff pastry

Láminas, fine slices

Mollejas, gizards of an animal

Paella, a traditional rice dish originating in the province of Valencia

This dish takes many forms and the following are some of the most popular. They usually include some vegetable but the final mix of supplementary ingredients varies according to the individual restaurants.

Paella marisco or **Paella marinera**, made with seafood

Paella Valenciana, made with chicken or/and rabbit

Paella de pollo, made with chicken

Paella mixta, made with a combination of chicken or pork and seafood

Paella/Arroz a la banda, cooked in a fish sauce

Pan, bread

Patatas fritas, chips

Patatas bravas, spicy potato chunks

Pesto, pesto sauce

Picadas or **para picar** nibbles (literally, something to pick at)

Picante, spicy

Piñones, pine nuts

Pisto, fried vegetable hash

Plato, dish or plate

Plato combinado, a full meal on one plate which usually consists of meat, fries and salad or sometimes an egg

Plato de carne a la parilla, mixed grill

Plato especial, special house dish

Por encargo, special order

Postre, dessert

Propina, tip

Rebozado/a, coated in breadcrumbs with egg**Un relleno de**, a stuffing of

Rellenos/as de, stuffed with

Revuelto, scrambled

Salsa, sauce

Salteado, sautéed

Servicio no incluido, service charge (tip) not included

Servicio incluido, tip included

Servido con, served with

Servieta, napkin (paper or otherwise according to the restaurant)

Surtido, assorted (e.g. *surtido de postres*, assorted desserts)

Tierno/a, tender

Tabla de quesos, cheeseboard

Tapas, tasty snacks (lit. fillers)

Tapas variadas, a selection of tapas

Wine (*Vino*) - basic vocabulary

Una botella de vino, a bottle of wine

Copa de vino, glass of wine

Jarra de vino, carafe or jug of wine

Vino tinto, red wine

Vino blanco, white wine

Vino rosado, rosé

Vino de la casa, house wine

Vino dulce, sweet wine

Vino seco, dry wine

Vino frio, cold wine (in summer, red wine is sometimes served cold)*Vino de tiempo*, means wine at room temperature. *Templado* is also sometimes used.

Vino joven, young wine for drinking now

Crianza, wine aged for 2 years with 6 months minimum in oak barrels

Reserva, wine aged for 3 years with 12 months minimum in oak barrels

Gran Reserva, wine aged

for 5 years with a minimum of 24 months in oak.

If the label says *barrica* the wine has been matured in barrels. If the label states *roble,* the wine has been matured in oak barrels.

Cooking or preparation instructions

Common examples of instructions given on packaging that may prove useful

Modo de empleo, preparation method

Disolver el contenido del sobre en 1 litro de agua caliente (sin que llegue a hervir), y llevar a ebullición removiendo al mismo tiempo.

Disolve the contents of the packet in 1 litre of hot water (without reaching boiling point), and bring to boiling point whilst stirring at the same time.

Verter 1 litro de agua en un recipiente adecuado para microondas. Añadir el contenido del sobre, remover bien y colocar en el microonda remover bien y colocar en el microonda at 800 watts durante 10 minutos.

Pour 1 litre of water In a container suitable for microwaves. Add the contents of the packet, stir well and place in the microwave at 800 watts for 10 minutes.

Remover y dejar reposar 2 minutos. Servir.

Stir and allow to rest for 2 minutes. Serve.

Verter el contenido del sobre en 1 litro de agua fria, remover y llevarlo a ebullición.

Empty the contents of the packet in 1 litre of cold water, stir and bring it almost to boiling point.

Tapar parcialmente y dejar cocer a fuego lento durante 10 minutos, removiendo de vez en cuando.

Partially cover and cook over a low heat for 10 minutes; stir occasionally.*Llene un recipiente con 1 litro de agua y cuando esté herviendo, veirta el contenido del sobre, removiendo constantemente hasta su completa disolución.*

Fill a container with 1 litre of water and when it is boiling, add the contents of the packet, stirring constantly until completely dissolved.

Añada directamente congelados a la sartén o freidora

con abundante aceite muy caliente y fríarlos hasta se doran al gusto (3 minutos). Si desea reducir el contenido de grasa del producto, escúrralo bien y colóquelo unos instantes sobre una servilleta de papel absorbente.

Add directly from frozen to the frying pan or deep fryer with plenty of very hot oil until golden according to taste (3 minutes). If you wish to reduce the fat content of the product, drain well and place on an absorbant paper serviette for a few moments.

Verter el contenido en 2 litros de agua herviendo salada. Cuando vuelva a hervir, cocer 4 minutos a fuego moderado. Escurrir y accompañar con la salsa deseada.

Empty the contents into 2 litres of boiling, salted water;when it returns to boiling, cook for 4 minutes over medium heat. Drain and accompany with your desired sauce.

Recurring vocabulary in Spanish cooking instructions:

Cocer, cook

Cocción, cooking

Colocar / coloque, place or put

Descongelar, thaw, *sin descongelar*, without thawing

Disolver, disolve, disuelto, disolved

Escurrir, drain, (*escúrrelo,* drain it)

Freidora, fryer (deep)

Fuego, flame or heat

Fuego lento, slow heat

Hervir, boil, (*herviendo*, boiling)

Recipiente, container (saucepan, jug, mixing bowl etc.)

Remover, to stir,

removiendo, stirring

Sarten, frying pan

Ola de presión, pressure cooker

Verter, pour, or put into, or empty into, eg. a container/ or saucepan

Section 2: English - Spanish

Fish - *Pescado*

anchovy, *Anchoa o boquerones*

bass or **sea bass**, *Lubina*

bream, *Dorada*

brine, *Salmuera* **or** *agua salada natural*

cod, *Bacalao*

Dover sole, *lenguado*

eel, *anguila*

grouper, *mero*

hake, *merluza*

herring, *arenque*

kipper, *arenque ahumado*

mackeral, *caballa*

monkfish, *rape*

pilchards, *sardinas*

salmon, *salmón*

sardines, *Sardinas*

sea bream, *Mojarra*

shrimps, *Camerones*

sole, *Lenguado*

swordfish, *Emperador* **or** *Pez espada*

trout, *Trucha*

tuna, *Atún,* also known as *bonito*

tuna in sunflower oil, *Atún en aceite girasol*

tuna in vegetable oil, *Atún en aceite vegetal*

turbot, *Rodaballo*

whitebait, *Chanquetes* **or** *moralla*

whiting, *Pescadilla*

Sea Food and shellfish - *Mariscos*

baby cuttlefish, *Chiperones*

baby squids, *Chopitos*

clam, *Almeja*

cockles, *Berberechos*

coquille St. Jacques, *Vieira en salsa preparada en concha*

crab, *Cangrejo*

crab, *Buey del mar*

crayfish, *Cigalas*

cuttlefish, *Sepia*

eel, *Anguila (*tiny eels are called *angula* and a typical regional dish Is called *gula*)

fish roe, *Huevas*

goose barnacles, *Percebes*

large red prawns, *Carabineros*

lobster, *Langosta,* (see also *Bogavante*)

lobster, *Bogavante*

mussels, *Mejillones*

oysters, *Ostras*

octopus, *Pulpo*

prawns, *Gambas*

king prawns, *Gambón gigante*

peeled prawns, *Gambas peladas*

uncooked prawns, *Gambas crudas*

cooked prawns, *Gambas cocidas*

razor (shell) fish, *Navajas*

sea urchin, *Erizo*

scallop, *Vieira***squid**, *Calamar*

squid fried in batter, *Calamar a la romana*

Poultry - *Aves, Pollería*

Chicken, *pollo*, **Duck**, *pato*, **Turkey**, *pavo.*

Examples given below are for chicken cuts i.e. *pollo*. For duck or turkey cuts, simply substitute one of the words above.

Chicken wings, *alas de pollo*

Chicken breast, *Pechuga de pollo*

Chicken thighs, *Entremusculos de pollo*

Chicken liver, *Hígado de pollo*

Chicken legs, *Jamoncitos de pollo*

Boneless chicken thighs, *Entremusculos de pollo sin hueso*

Chicken breast , *Pechuga de pollo)*

Roast chicken, *Pollo asado*

Whole chicken breast, *Pechuga de pollo entera*

Whole chicken, *Pollo entero*

Chicken leg quarters, *Traseros de pollo*

Whole oven ready chicken, *Pollo entero limpio*

Skinless, *Sin piel*

Goose, *oca*

Hen, *Gallina*

Pheasant, *Faisán*

Partridge, *perdiz*

Quails, *codornices*

Beef - Ternera

beef, *Ternera*

beef burgers, *Hamburguesas de ternera*

beef for frying, *Ternera para freir*

beef joint, *Tenera para asar*

beef meatballs, *Albondigas de ternera*

beef sausages, *Salchichas de ternera*

beef ribs, *Costillas de ternera*

beef steak, *Bistec*

corned beef, *Tenera en lata*

cow, *Vaca*

entrecote, *Entrecote*

fillet steak, *Filete de ternera*

minced beef, *Ternera picada*

ox tail, *Rabo de buey*

ox tongue, *legua de buey*

roast beef, *Rosbif*

stewing steak, *Ternera para guisar*

tripe, *Callos*

Pork and Ham - *Cerdo y Jamón*

bacon, *Bacón* sometimes spelled *beicon*

belly pork, *Panceta de cerdo*

chopped pork, *cerdo troceado*

Ham, *Jamón*

ham off the bone, *Jamón de la pata*. Sometimes called *jamón al horno*

ham off the bone, may be labelled *lacón* in supermarket pre-packs

Iberian ham, *Jamón Iberico*

Iberian shoulder pork, *Paleta Ibérica*

loin cuts, *Magro*

pig's kidneys, *Riñones de cerdo*

pig's liver, *Higado de cerdo*

pig's trotters, *patas de cerdo* **or** *codillo de cerdo*

pork, *Cerdo*

pork chops, *Chuletas de cerdo*

pork joint, *Cerdo para asar*

pork loin, *Lomo de cerdo*

pork meatballs, *Albondigas de cerdo*

chopped pork, *cerdo troceado*

ham off the bone, may be labelled *lacón* in supermarket pre-packs

Iberian shoulder pork, *Paleta Ibérica*

loin cuts, *Magro*

pig's kidneys, *Riñones de cerdo*

pig's liver, *Higado de cerdo*

pig's trotters, *patas de cerdo* **or** *codillo de cerdo*

pork, *Cerdo*

pork chops, *Chuletas de cerdo*

pork joint, *Cerdo para asar*

pork loin, *Lomo de cerdo*

pork meatballs, *Albondigas de cerdo*

pork mince, *Cerdo picada*

pork ribs, *Costillas de cerdo*

pork sausages, *Salchichas de cerdo*

rashers, *Lonchas de bacón*

Serrano ham, *Jamón Serrano*

shoulder cut pork chops, *Chuletas de aguja*

shoulder pork off the bone, *Lacón*

skewered pieces of marinaded pork, *Pincho moruno*

smoked bacon, *Bacón ahumado*

spam, *Cerdo procesado*

York ham, *Jamón York*

Lamb - *Cordero*

lamb, *Cordero*

lamb chops, *Chuletas de cordero*

lamb breast, *Pechuga de cordero*

lamb joint, *Cordero para asar*

leg of lamb *o* **leg shanks**, *Pierna de cordero*

lamb breast, *Pechuga de cordero*

minced lamb, *Cordero picado*

mutton, *Cordero maduro*

neck of lamb, *Cuello de cordero*

Prepared Meats - *Carnes Preparadas*

black pudding, *Morcilla*

Chorizo, chorizo

corned beef, *Ternera en lata*

luncheon meat, *cerdo en lata*

meat on a skewer, *Pinchos morunos*

pork sausage made with spices, *Longaniza*

ready to cook on the barbeque, *Preparados barbacoa*

spicy sausage similar to salami, *Salchichón*

hot dog, *perrito*

Vegetables - *Verduras*

Artichoke, *Alcachofa*

Aubergine, *Berenjena*

Avocado, *Aguacate*

Asparagus, *Espárragos*

Beans, *Alubias*

beetroot, *Remolacha*

broad beans, *Habas*

broccoli, *Brecól*

Brussel sprouts, *Repollito de Bruselas (*or simply *Bruselas)*

Butter beans, *alubias blancas* or *garrofón*

cabbage, *Col o repollo*

carrot, *Zanahoria*

cauliflower, *Coliflor*

Celery, *Apio*

Courgette, *Calabacín*

cucumber, *Pepino*

dried beans *o* **haricote**, *Frijoles*

endive, *Endiva*

gherkins, *Pepinillos*

green beans, *Judias-*

runner beans, *judias planas*

- **french beans**, *judias redondas*

green pepper, *Pimiento verde*

leek, *Puerro*

lettuce, *Lechuga*

mushrooms, *Champiñones*

Olives, *Aceitunas*

Onion, *Cebolla*

peas, *Guisantes*

potato, *Patata*

red pepper, *Pimiento rojo*

spring onion, *Cebolla tierna*

spinach, *Espinacas*

sweet corn, *Maiz dulce* **or** *maiz tierno*

swede, *Nabo sueco*

Swiss chard, *Acelgas*

Tomato, *Tomate*

turnip, *Nabo*

vegetables, *Verduras* (in general)

Fruit - *Fruta*

Apple, *Manzana*

Apricot, *Albericoque*

Banana, *Plátano*

Blackberry, *Mora*

Blackcurrent, *grosella negra*

Cherry, *Cereza*

Cranberry, *Arándano*

Damson, *Ciruela damascena*

Date, *datil*

Fig, *higo*

Gooseberry, *Grosella espinosa*

Grape, *Uva*

Grapefruit, *Pomelo*

Grapefruit, also known as *Toronja*

Kiwi, *kiwi*

Lemon, *Limón*

Lime, *Lima*

Melon, *Melón*

Nectarine, *Nectarina*

Orange, *Naranja*

Peach, *Melocotón*

Pear, *Pera*

Pineapple, *Piña*

Plum, *Ciruela*

Prunes, *ciruela secada*

Strawberry, *Fresa*

Raisins, *pasas*

Rasberry, *Frambuesa*

Redcurrant, *Grosella*

Strawberry, *Fresa*

Watermelon, *Sandía*

Rice and Beans - *Arrozes y Alubias*

Beans, *Alubias*

baked beans, *Alubias cocidas*

broad beans, *Habas*

butter beans, *Alubias blancas*

chickpea, *Garbanzo*

green beans, *Judias*

haricot beans, *Frijoles*

lentils, *Lentejas*

rice, *Arroz*

- **long grain rice**, *Arroz de grano largo*

- **round grain rice**, *Arroz redondo*

- **whole grain rice**, *Arroz integral*

Bakery - *Panadería*

Baguette, *Barra*

- **wholemeal baguette**, *Barra integral*

- **with seeds**, *Con semillas*

- **with sesame seeds**, *Con semillas sésamo*

bread, *Pan*

- **bread without crust** *o* **crustless bread**, *Pan sin corteza*

- **bread roll** *o* **bun** *o* **bap**, *Panecillo*

- **granary bread**, *de trigo, centeno y cebada*

- **loaf of bread**, *Pan de molde*

- **milk bread**, *Pan de leche*

- **rye bread**, de centeno

- **sliced bread**, *Pan cortado-*

wholemeal bread, *Pan integral*

cake, *Pastel* **or** *dulce*

croissant, *Croisant*

Pasty, *Empanadilla*

- **meat pasty**, *empanadilla de carne*

-**spinach pasty**, *empanadilla de espinacas*

Pie, *Tarta*

- **meat pie**, *Tarta de carne*

Puff pastry, *Hojaldre*

tart, *tarta*, e.g. **apple tart**, *tarta de manzana*

Steak an kidney pie, *Tarta de ternera y riñon*

Wheatgerm, *germen de trigo*

Cakes - dulces

Biscuits, *galletas*

Custard, *natilla*

Flan, *flan*

Ice cream, *helado*

Ice lolly, *polo*

Jelly, *gelatina*

Pancake, *tortita dulce or crepe*

Pie, *tarta*

Pudding, *Budín o Pudín*

Sponge or a confection similar, *bizcocho*

Tart, *tarta*

Truffles, *trufas*

Dairy Foods

butter, *Mantequilla*

- **salted butter** , *Mantequilla con sal*

- **unsalted butter**, *Mantequilla sin sal*

cheese, *Queso*

- **grated cheese**, *queso rallado*

- **grated**, *queso gratinado* **or** *queso en polvo*

cream, *Nata*

- **pouring cream** *nata para montar*

- **cooking cream**, *nata para cocinar*

- **sour cream**. *nata para cocinar*

whipped cream, *nata montada*

eggs, *huevos*

- **free range eggs**, *huevos camperos*

milk, *leche*

milk, *leche*

- whole milk, *leche entera*

- semi-skimmed milk, *leche semi-desnatada*

- skimmed milk, *leche desnatada*

- calcium enriched milk, *leche con calcio*

- condensed milk, *leche condensada*

- goat's milk, *de cabra-*

- sheep's milk, *de oveja*

yoghurt, *yogur*

Related vocabulary

Blue, *azul*

Cured, *curado*

- semi-cured, *semi-curado*

creamed *o* **creamy**, *cremoso*

for spreading, *de untar*

hard, *duro*

mild, *o* **tender**, *tierno/a*

mixed o mixture, *mezcla*

slices, *lonchas*

strong flavour, *sabor intenso*

with herbs, *con hierbas*

with nuts, *con nueces*

Spices - *Especias*

Basil, *Albahaca*

bay leaf, *Laurel*

cardamom, *Cardamomo*

chilli, *Chili*

chilli powder, *Chili en polvo*

- hot chilli, *chili picante*

cinnamon, *Canela*

cinnamon stick, *Canela en rama*

cloves, *Clavos*

coriander, *Cilantro*

cumin seeds, *Cominos*

dill, *Enaldo*

garlic, *Ajo (diente de ajo* - **garlic clove**)

- **powdered garlic,** *Ajo en polvo*

ginger, *Ginebre*

mixed herbs (with a hint of mint), *Hierba buena*

mint, *Menta*

Mixed herbs (Provence), *Hierbas provencales*

mustard, *Mostaza*

nutmeg, *Nuez moscada*

Oregano, *Orégano*

paprika, *Pimentón*

- **hot paprika**, *Pimentón picante*

Parsley, *Perejil*

Pepper, *Pimienta*

-black pepper, *Pimienta negra*

Peppercorns, *Pimienta en grano*

rosemary, *Romero*

saffron, *Azafrán*

sage, *Salvia*

table salt, *Sal de mesa*

tarragon, *Estragón*

thyme, *Tomillo*

turmeric, *Cúrcuma*

Nuts - *Nueces*

Almonds, *Almendras*

Brazil nut, *Coquito, or Nuez de Brasil*

Cashew, *Anacardo*

Chestnuts, *Castañas*

Coconut, *Coco*

Hazelnut, *Avellana*

Macadamia, *Macadamia*

Peanuts, *Cacahuetes*

Pecan, *Pecana*

Pistachio, *Pistacho*

Salted, *Con sal*

Toasted or **roasted**, *Tostado*

Walnut, *nogal*

Drinks and Refreshments - *Bebidas y Refrescos*

a glass of ...(insert alcholic drink), *una copa de*....normally used when you order an alcholic drink.

- a glass is also called *un vaso* when you order a non-alcholic drink

beer, *Cerveza*

- beer from a barrel, *Caña*

- Lager, *Cerveza (estilo Alemán)*

- non-alcoholic beer, *Cerveza sin alcohol*

coffee, *Café*

- black coffee, *Café Americano*

- coffee with milk *o* white coffee, *Café con leche*

- decaffinated coffee, *Café descafelnudo*

- espresso, *Café espresso*

cup, *Taza*

Juice, *zumo*

- **squeezed orange juice**, *Zumo de naranja exprimido*

milk, *Leche*

- **soya milk**, *leche de soja*

milkshake, *Batido*

refreshment, *Refresco*

tea, *Té*

 - **green tea,** *té verde*

- **chamomile tea**, *Infusión de manzanilla*

- **lime blossom tea**, *Infusion de tila*

Water, *Agua*

- **fizzy water**, *Agua con gas*

- **spring water,** *Agua de manantial*

- **still water**, *Agua sin gas*

wine, *Vino*

- **white wine**, *Vino blanco*

- **rosé wine**, *Vino rosado*

- **red wine**, *Vino tinto*

- **house wine**, *Vino de la casa*

- **dry wine**, *Vino seco*

- **sweet wine**, *Vino dulce*

- **semi dry wine**, *Vino semi-seco*

- **demi-sec**, vino semi seco

Related vocabulary

carafe or jug, *Jarra*

cold, *Frío*

hot, *Caliente*

very milky, *Largo de leche*

strong coffee white coffee,*café con leche largo de café*

warm, *Templado*

with ice, *Con hiélo*

without ice, *Sin hielo*

In the Supermarket - *Supermercado*

baking powder, *Levadura*

best before…..(date), *Consumir preferentemente antes de…..*

bitter, *Amarga*

broth, *caldo* **or** *sopa*

can, *lata*

conserve, *mermelada*

contains nuts, *Contiene nuezes*

cooked, *Cocido/a*

cured, *curado/a*

custard, *natilla*

dressing, *Aliño*

easy to open, *Abre fácil***eat before… (date)**, *Fecha de caducidad….*

fat, *Grasa*

low in fat, *Bajo en grasa*

flakes or shreds, migas

flour (plain), *Harina de trigo*

- self-raising flour, *harina con levadura*

hash, *Picadillo*

- hash browns, *Picadillo de patata*

gluten free, *sin gluten*

- contains gluten, *Contiene gluten*

gravy, *Salsa de carne*

hot & spicy, *Picante* (but not usually as strong as in curries)

jam, *Mermelada*

lunch, *Almuerzo o comida*

marmalade, *Mermelada de naranja*

microwave, *Micro onda*

noodles, *Tallerines*

olive oil, *Aceite de oliva*

once opened store in refridgerator, una vez abierta, conservar en nevera.

open here, *Abre acqui*

oven cooked, cocido *al horno*

peeled, *Pelado*

pickle, *Escabache*

portion, *trozo o ración para una persona*

ration, *Ración*

relish, *salsa gourmet***sauce**, *Salsa*

self-raising flour, *harina con levadura*

sell by date…., *vender antes del…*

serving, *ración*

shreds, *migas*

skewers, *Brochetas*

slices, *Lonchas*

- thin slices, *Lonchas finas*

- thick slices, *Lonchas gordas*

slice (e.g. of cake), *Trozo* **or** *trozito*

smoked, *Ahumado/a*

soup, *sopa*

spread, *Untar*

steamed, *al vapor*

stir fry, *Sofreir***stock**, *Caldo*

- stock or **dehydrated soup**, *Caldito*

store in a cool, dry place, *Conservar en lugar fresco y seco*

stuffed, *Rellenado*

stuffing, *relleno*

sunflower oil, *Aceite de girasol*

sun dried, *Secado al sol*

sweet & sour sauce, *Salsa agridulce*

tin, *lata*

top down (as in sauce bottles etc.), *boca abajo*

vacuum packed, *Envasado al vacio*

vinegar, *Vinagre*

wheat, *Trigo*

without artificial colourings, *Sin colorantes artificiales*

without artificial preservatives, *Sin conservantes artificiales*

Restaurant - *Restaurante*

Handy phrases

the menu please, *La carta por favor*

dish of the day, *Menu* or *plato del día* (the 'menu' as we know it in English is usually *la carta* in most restaurants, similar to the French phrase *á la carte* often used in English restaurants)

a table for 2 (3, 4 etc.), *Una mesa para 2 (3, 4 etc.)*

(one, *uno,* **two,** *dos,* **three,** *tres,* **four,** *cuatro,* **five,** *cinco,* **six,** *seis,* **seven,** *siete,* **eight,** *ocho,* **nine,** *nueve,* **ten,** *diez.)*

I want to reserve a table, *Quiero reservar una mesa*

at eight o'clock (at nine o'clock etc.), *A las ocho,(a las nueve etc.)*

the bill please, *La cuenta por favo*

*r***I'll pay with a credit card**, *Pago con tarjeta*

A knife and fork please, *Una cubierta por favor* *(cubierta* is the collective word for the usual eating utensils). The individual items are: **Knife** - *cuchillo,* **Fork** - *tenedor,* **Spoon** - *cuchara.*

A plate please, *un plato por favor*

waiter/waitress, *Camarero/a*

Useful vocabulary commonly found on menus. This is not a comprehensive list because the inventiveness of restaurants throughout the world produces dishes with names that will not be found in any dictionary. However, some of this vocabulary may prove useful at the dinner table. The basic ingredients of meals may be found in the Supermarket food section.

appetizers or hors d'ouvres, *entremeses*

au gratin, *gratinado* (usually a topping of breadcrumbs and cheese)

baked, *al horno*

barbecued, *A la barbacoa*

bread, *pan*

breakfast, *desayuno*

casserole, *Cazuela*

chargrilled, *A la brasa*

cheeseboard, *Tabla de quesos*

chips, *Patatas fritas*

coated in batter (breadcrumbs with egg), *Rebozado/a*

cooked in cider, *A la sidra*

creamed cheese, *crema de queso*

crisps (in packets), *patatas fritas (laminadas en paquete)*

crispy or crunchy, *crujiente*

dessert, *postre.* **A selection of desserts,** *surtido de postres*

appetizers or hors d'ouvre, *entremeses*

french fries, *patatas fritas   recien hechas*

fresh bread, *pan recien hecho* **or** *recien hornado* **or** *pan fresco*

fine slices, *láminas*

with garlic, *Al ajillo (garlic, ajo)*

garnishing, *guarnación*

grilled, *A la parilla*

grilled on a hot plate, *A la plancha*

home made, *casero/a*

mixed grill, *plato de carne a la parilla* (a selection of meats which may consist of chops, sausages, spare ribs, etc.)

napkin, *Servieta de tela*

nibbles, *Picadas* or *para picar*

pesto sauce, *pesto*

pine nuts, *piñones*

puff pastry, *hojaldre*

regional dish, *Comida típica*

rabbit, *Conejo*

roasted, *Asado*

scrambled, *Revuelto*

sauce, *salsa*

sautéed, *Salteado*

service charge (tip) not included, *Servicio no incluido*

service charge (tip) included, *Servicio incluido*

served with, *servido con*

serviette, servieta**special order,** *Por encargo*

starters, *Entrantes*

stew, *Estofado*

stuffing, *relleno*

tender, *tierno/a*

tip, *Propina*

venison, *Venado*

well done, *Bien hecho*, **or** *bien cocido*

N.B. some restaurants serve a *plato combinado* which is basically a meal on one plate. This can consist of meat, egg and fries.depending on the restaurant

<u>Wine</u> (*Vino*) - Basic essentials

a bottle of wine, *Una botella de vino*

dry wine, *vino seco*

carafe or jug of wine, *una jarra de vino*

sweet wine, *vino dulce*

half bottle, *Media botella*

glass of wine, *Copa de vino*

matured in oak, *Crianza   (en roble)*

red wine, *Vino tinto*

white wine, *Vino blanco*

rosé, *Vino rosado*

house wine, *Vino de la casa*

N.B. If you are unfortunate enough to be served wine that is corked, the phrase to use is, **el *vino pica***. You could also say, **el *vino no está bien*** (the wine is not good)

This is the end of this edition; we hope this helps you enjoy your eating experience in Spain. If you found it useful, please recommend it to a friend. Thank you and happy eating, or, as the Spanish might say, **'*Buen proveche*'**.

The author's book about life experience in Spain, **Reach for the Sun**, is available on Amazon Kindle.

http://www.amazon.com/dp/B008TAFL2K

For those interested in regional languages the following is the original Galician text of the Queimada Incantation

Mouchos, curuxas, sapos e bruxas.

Demos, trasgos e diaños,

espíritos das neboadas veigas.

Corvos, píntegas e meigas:

feitizos das menciñeiras.

Podres cañotas furadas,

fogar dos vermes e alimañas.

Lume das Santas Compañas,

mal de ollo, negros meigallos,

cheiro dos mortos, tronos e raios.

Ouveo do can, pregón da morte;

fuciño do sátiro e pé do coello.

Pecadora   lingua da mala muller

casada cun home vello.

Averno de Satán e Belcebú,

lume dos cadáveres ardentes,

corpos mutilados dos indecentes,

peidos dos infernais cus,

muxido da mar embravecida.

Barriga inútil da muller solteira,

falar dos gatos que andan á
xaneira,

Guedella porca da cabra mal
parida.

Con este fol levantarei

as chamas deste lume

que asemella ao do Inferno,

e fuxirán as bruxas

a cabalo das súas vasoiras,

índose bañar na praia

das areas   gordas.

¡Oíde, oíde! os ruxidos

que dan as que non poden

deixar de queimarse no
augardente

quedando así purificadas.

E cando este beberaxe

baixe polas nosas gorxas,

quedaremos libres dos males

da nosa alma e de todo
embruxamento.

Forzas do ar, terra, mar e lume,

a vós fago esta chamada:

se é verdade que tendes máis
poder

que a humana xente,

eiquí e agora, facede que os
espíritos

dos amigos que están fóra,

participen con nós desta
Queimada

Printed in Great Britain
by Amazon

16732482R00072